MY CANADA

MANITOBA

Weigl

Published by Weigl Educational Publishers Limited
6325 10th Street SE
Calgary, Alberta T2H 2Z9

Website: www.weigl.ca

Library and Archives Canada Cataloguing in Publication

Goldsworthy, Kaite, author
      Manitoba / Kaite Goldsworthy.

(My Canada)
ISBN 978-1-77071-866-1 (bound).
ISBN 978-1-77071-867-8 (pbk.)

      1. Manitoba--Juvenile literature. I. Title. II. Series: My Canada
(Calgary, Alta.)

FC3361.2.G65 2013   j971.27   C2013-902393-3

Printed in the United States of America in North Mankato, Minnesota
1 2 3 4 5 6 7 8 9 0   17 16 15 14 13

052013
WEP040413

Project Coordinator: Megan Cuthbert
Art Director: Terry Paulhus

Weigl acknowledges Getty Images as the primary image supplier for this title.

We acknowledge the financial support of the Government of Canada through the Canada Book Fund for our publishing activities.

Contents

This is Manitoba. The name comes from an Ojibwe word that means Great Spirit.

4

This is the shape of Manitoba. Nunavut is north of Manitoba. The United States borders Manitoba.

Saskatchewan and Ontario sit on each side of Manitoba.

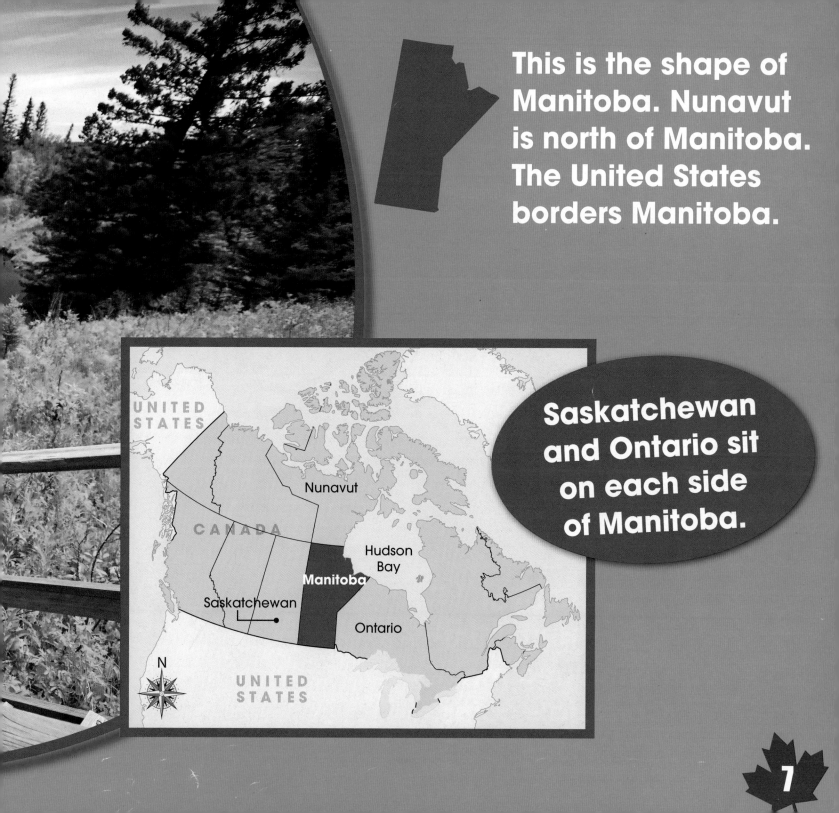

UNITED
STATES

Nunavut

CANADA

Hudson
Bay

Manitoba

Saskatchewan

Ontario

N

UNITED
STATES

Winnipeg is the capital city of Manitoba. The Forks is a place in Winnipeg where the Red and Assiniboine Rivers meet.

The Royal Canadian Mint in Winnipeg makes Canada's coins.

People came to Manitoba to trade for fur. They worked with First Nations people to find furs.

Beaver fur was used to make hats.

The province's coat of arms has a green shield with a bison on a rock. A unicorn, beaver, and white horse surround the shield.

GLORIOSUS · ET · LIBER

A beaver's teeth never stop growing. Chewing on wood helps keep its teeth from getting too long.

This is the flag of Manitoba. It is red with the flag of Great Britain in the top corner. The shield is on the right.

The main symbol on the shield is a bison. Large herds of bison used to live throughout Manitoba.

The great grey owl is Manitoba's official bird. It is the largest owl in North America. Grey owls live in the forests of the province.

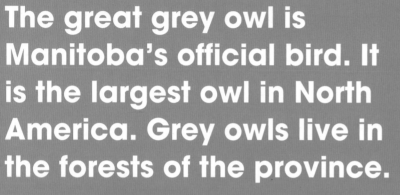

The flower of Manitoba is the prairie crocus. It grows on the prairies and in open woods.

Manitoba has many rivers. The province uses water from its rivers to make electricity.

Dams on the rivers help make electricity.

Thousands of people visit Churchill every year. It is called the "Polar Bear Capital of the World."

People can take tours to see polar bears that live near the town.

MANITOBA FACTS

These pages provide detailed information that expands on the interesting facts found in the book. These pages are intended to be used by adults as a learning support to help young readers round out their knowledge of each province and territory in the *My Canada* series.

Pages 4–5

The Ojibwe named the area "great spirit" because they thought the sound of the water in the lakes was the sound of a great spirit. Manitoba is 647,797 square kilometers and has a population of about 1.2 million people. It is called the "Land of 100,000 Lakes." All rivers in Manitoba flow to Hudson Bay.

Pages 6–7

Manitoba is the most eastern of the prairie provinces. It is in the centre of eastern and western Canada and is often called the "Keystone Province" because it is central. The northeast of the province borders Hudson Bay. Lake Winnipeg is the largest lake in the province and the 10th largest freshwater lake in the world. It covers nearly four percent of the province.

Pages 8–9

Approximately 700,000 people live in Winnipeg. It was incorporated as a city in 1873. The Forks was the site of many early fur trading forts such as Fort Garry, Fort Rouge, and Fort Gibraltar. The Canadian coins in circulation are all made at the Royal Canadian Mint in Winnipeg. More than one billion coins are produced each year.

Pages 10–11

The area around Hudson Bay was settled by people looking for a passage through the north to Asia. In 1670, King Charles of England gave the land around the bay to the Hudson's Bay Trading Company. The company set up many fur trading posts in the area. The soft underfur, or felt, of beaver pelts was used to make hats in the 18th and 19th centuries, until silk hats became popular.

Pages 12–13

The unicorn on Manitoba's shield is from the coat of arms of England and Scotland. The white horse is included because it was important to the First Nations, the Métis, and European settlers. The motto at the bottom is "glorious and free." At the top of the shield is the flag of England. The beaver is known for its buck teeth and flat tail.

Pages 14–15

The Manitoba flag is similar to the Red Ensign, which was the official flag of Canada until 1965. Manitoba's flag also features the provincial shield of arms. The Union Jack refers to the history of Manitoba, and Canada, as a British colony. Bison were a major source of food and clothing for the First Nations people and early settlers of Manitoba.

Pages 16–17

The great grey owl became Manitoba's official bird in 1987. The owl lives in the province year round. It has a wingspan of 1.5 metres. Great grey owls can spot prey as far as 200 metres away. The prairie crocus grows very early in the spring. The entire plant is covered in hairs. It is poisonous if eaten, causing blisters and inflammation.

Pages 18–19

Manitoba has 14 hydroelectric stations that generate almost all the electricity for the province. The stations can generate 5,499 megawatts of electricity. Energy is produced when water flows through turbines inside dams. Extra electricity is sold to the rest of Canada and the United States.

Pages 20–21

Churchill is located on the southwest edge of Hudson Bay and the mouth of the Churchill River. Approximately 800 people live there. There are no roads, so visitors must travel by train or plane. Polar bears generally move through town in October and November. There are approximately 1,200 polar bears in the Churchill area.

KEY WORDS

Research has shown that as much as 65 percent of all written material published in English is made up of 300 words. These 300 words cannot be taught using pictures or learned by sounding them out. They must be recognized by sight. This book contains 56 common sight words to help young readers improve their reading fluency and comprehension. This book also teaches young readers several important content words, such as proper nouns. These words are paired with pictures to aid in learning and improve understanding.

Page	Sight Words First Appearance
4	an, comes, from, great, is, means, name, that, the, this, word
7	and, each, of, on, side
8	a, city, in, makes, place, rivers, where
11	came, find, for, people, they, to, used, was, with
12	has, white
13	helps, its, keep, long, never, stop, too
15	it, large, live, right
17	grows, open
19	many, water
20	can, every, near, see, take, world, year

Page	Content Words First Appearance
4	Manitoba, Ojibwe, spirit
7	Hudson Bay, Nunavut, Ontario, Saskatchewan, shape, United States
8	Canada, coins, The Forks, Royal Canadian Mint, Winnipeg
11	beaver, First Nations, fur, hats
12	bison, coat of arms, horse, province, rock, shield, unicorn
13	teeth, wood
15	corner, flag, Great Britain, herds, symbol, top
16	bird, forests, owl, North America
17	flower, prairie crocus, prairies
19	dams, electricity
20	capital, Churchill, polar bear, thousands, tours, town

WEBSITES

To learn more about Manitoba, visit these websites.

Manitoba Government
http://www.gov.mb.ca

Citizens and Immigration Canada
http://www.cic.gc.ca/english/games/teachers-corner/fact-sheet-manitoba.asp

Travel Manitoba
http://www.travelmanitoba.com/ArtsAndCulture/HistoryMuseums/BigPicture/ManitobaFunFacts/